Life in the Eyes of an Autistic Person

Alexander Hubbard

Alexander Hubbard

10/12/2013

For my mother Linda Hubbard,
that takes care of me as I take care of her.

Contents

Alexander Hubbard's Introduction

I was born in Seattle, Washington on May 23rd, 1993 at Group Health Hospital; I have Autism and lives with my parents, older brother and younger sister. I was diagnosed with Asperger's Syndrome at the age of 3; I was born a blue baby. My race is Black/African American and part Native. I like to write stories; draw and sketch pictures, make friends and money, talking with people, I had had pets like dogs, cats, and guinea-pigs, I like to meet new people, rap and sing, act and make my own TV shows, and I like to watch TV and movies.

I feel happy when I do things, I feel bored when he has nothing to do and is sitting around the house. I feel upset if I not get what I want, and I get mad if something happens. I talk well with others. But I have a hard time communicating with others sometimes. I like to learn how to do math and get better at it. I want to keep my education going.

I graduated from The Center School on June 16th, 2011 and I completed my credits on June 15th, 2012. I will be attending to a transition program on September 2012; also maybe he might go to Seattle Central Community College. He will stay in school until he's 21. Alex is smart and he wants to be regular like everyone else. He wasn't allowed to going out at night, because his mom was afraid that he would get hurt and she would be worried. Alex got along with his parents often when he was younger, sometimes he didn't.

Alex doesn't like to get in trouble, being to mean to people, and being ignored by others. He wants to be an actor when he grows up. Alex gets angry when his parents and teachers tell him what to do. He likes to help people and do things with them. His brain told him many things that he wanted to do. Alex likes to do something he wants and make everyone happy.

Alex went to an internship called XIP, which stands for Exploratory Internship Program. He worked at the mailroom, he sorted and bundled mail during 1st semester on September 2010 'til January 2011. Also, he delivered mail during 2nd semester on February 2011 'til June 2011. Alex also worked at STAR Center for an internship, he already knows about computers. He learned new things from STAR Center during 1st semester on September 2011 'til January 2012. Also, he worked at SHAG Terrace during 2nd semester. He showed the seniors how to use new computers. After Alex worked at SHAG, he got transferred back to STAR Center and worked as a receptionist. Alex always did well at his internship.

Chapter One
My Childhood

When I was a baby, I sat on the grass by my grandmother's yard. I was in my crib crying a lot. At age three, I was diagnosed with a disability called Asperger's Syndrome. At age four, I was with my mom in the car, I was yelling and crying. My mom stopped the car and told me to stop it. So, I got out of the car and started running away while my mom ran after me and grabbed me. Then, she put me back in the car and told me to stop it again; I started to calm down. At age five, I wanted to meet the neighbors, but my mom said that I wasn't allowed to go out by myself. I like to walk around the block, but I have to get my mom's permission before I do that.

I started to learn how to write letters at the age of six. I have a hard time saying words, people don't understand what I saying and what I try to say. At the neighborhood, I was walking around, I said hi to the neighbors I didn't know, and they threatened me and tried to take my money, I was really scared. While visiting my grandmother, my mom's mother, I spent time with her. I also spent time with my grandfather, my aunt, uncles and cousins. My cousins like to play games with me.

They liked to pick on me when I was little. Every time I did something bad when I was with my cousins, they took out their belts and started whooping me up. I was crying a lot when I got whooped. My cousins were bad way back in my childhood. I think of the things that happened to me, when I was younger. When I said something rude to my aunt, she whooped me badly with her belt. I cried many times when I always got spanked by my family members.

Everyone thought I was cute when I was young, but I was very shy. I got along with my parents when I was really young. I went to the celebrations with my family and I enjoyed it sometimes.

I was about two years old in this picture; I was sitting on the chair with my bottle.

At age ten, when I was with my mom, we went places. I started getting angry when my mom and my older brother told me what to do. At age eleven, hit my mom many times when she didn't get something for me that I wanted. When I was about nine or ten, my sister and I, we had fun times together like walking around the neighborhood, go bowling, and went swimming. I always got sent to Children's Hospital when I was feeling crazy. At age eight, my family and I went to Pullman to visit my brother. He went to college at Washington State University. I liked to run fast when I was skinny at age seven. At Pullman, I ran slowly because I was fat.

While we were visiting at my grandmother's house, I got upset and had a meltdown in the kitchen. My mom warned me, "Stop it right now," when I was jumping up and down very hard. My grandmother told me the same thing. My mom and my grandmother left me alone while I was in the kitchen, I calmed myself down. My aunt came into the kitchen to check and see that I was okay. I went outside of my grandmother's house; I was still angry with my mom. I grabbed her wrists and she said, "Alex, let go of my wrists right now. You stop it right now." I let go of her wrists, I tried to hit her with my hands, but she grabbed them and told me to stop. I cried, cried, cried, and cried. After that, I calmed myself down again.

During November 2001, I saw a movie commercial of Harry Potter and the Sorcerer's Stone. I went to Alki on that day to be like Harry Potter and I made a paper wand. I like Harry Potter very much. I read a little bit of the novel about him. I saw the movie Harry Potter and the Sorcerer's Stone for the first time in theaters, it's a really interesting movie. Every time I think about Harry Potter, it makes me think of magic and fantasy. I've seen all of the Harry Potter movies, from start to finish; then to now. Harry Potter is my favorite character; I will remember him in my head the most.

That's me when I was playing outside in front of my grandmother's house at age 4.

When I was very younger, I went to many doctor appointments. The doctors wanted to give me my shots, but I was scared of a getting a shot. I don't like the needles. They gave me a shot and I was screaming. After they did that, I was crying really hard. When I was an infant the doctors put me on the doctor table. I was yelling and screaming when they gave me a shot on my butt. My sister saw me screaming, she screamed too. I was crying really loud after they did that to me. I also went to my dentist appointment, I've been there before. I was really scared to go to the dentist. The doctor was touching my tooth, I yelled. They took out my baby tooth; my gums were hurting really bad. When I felt pain, I always cried a lot.

I wanted to be a good person, but every time I saw bad things, they made me want to do bad things. When I was about six or eight years old, I started watching scary movies and they gave me nightmares. My mom told me that I wasn't allowed to watch scary movies. She said, "Scary movies will mess up your mind." I didn't understand what she was saying. I like to watch scary movies, but not often. I was too young to watch scary movies. I was too young to watch R-rated movies, which my mom won't let me watch either. I was always trying to be careful of what I watched; some things would make my mind think terrible thoughts.

So, my brother, my sister and I moved out with my mom. We left Seattle and moved to Renton. The apartment was called Madison Apartments; it was in between Renton and Fairwood. I missed Seattle, but I was getting used to living in an apartment.

I love spending time with my dad at his house; I love him, he is a good father. I don't like to be mean to my family and to people. I felt sad that I moved out of Seattle. I got angry with my mom when I didn't have money. Whenever I didn't have money, I went into my mom's purse and tried to steal her money from the BECU envelope. My mom caught me when I was trying to do that. I don't like to steal, but I did it when I was really young. I was snuck into my grandmother's purse; I took out twenty bucks and put it in my pocket. I stole something from the grocery store; no one saw me. I noticed that stealing was bad, I feel bad when I steal something. I did a wrong thing way back when I was seven. I decided to give my grandmother back her twenty bucks I stole from her. I told her that I was very sorry and that what I did was wrong.

At age ten, I thought of an idea for what I could do during the summer. I decided to have a Kool-Aid stand in front of the apartments we lived in. I got a few customers, but I didn't make a lot of money. I noticed that I didn't have enough customers around our apartment area. On September 2004, we moved out of the apartments in Renton and moved back to Seattle. I was glad that we moved back to my dad's house. During the summer of 2005, I did my Kool-Aid stand again in front of my house. I usually had a few customers come to my stand. I always love selling Kool-Aid in the summertime.

I was an angry child when we moved back to our old house. I threw a plate at my mom, which is something I shouldn't have done. I told my mom that I was sorry and said bad things to her many times. I also said sorry to my brother and my sister, since I did wrong things to them hours ago, they wanted me to give them space. Sometimes I wouldn't be sorry for the many bad things that I did. Some people said I wasn't too, when they were being rude to me.

When I was little, I would be in the bathroom many times. The problem was... I never was potty-trained. It was very hard for me to wipe my butt. I didn't know how to do it and I was really scared. I had my mom do it for me. But, she wanted me to do it on my own, but I couldn't. At age eight, I still couldn't do it and I was still scared. At age nine, I got a little potty-trained, but still couldn't do it. Age ten, I really got it, but not all the way. Age eleven, I got it, but I still needed some practice with it. Age twelve, I did it on my own and it worked alright. I definitely knew how to do it and I became potty trained.

Chapter Two
My Grade School Years

At age three, I attended preschool at Thurgood Marshall Elementary School. I met some new friends who had Autism in my old classroom. I got along with my teacher, the aids, and the students very well. While I was at Thurgood Marshall; I was really shy at that time because I had never met those people and never had been to school before. When I got to know all the students, I wanted to try to be on a good behavior. Whenever I touch something by the kitchen area and the door, the teacher told me not to touch anything I shouldn't be touching. I liked to touch things when I was young, but I usually touched people and they told me that I wasn't allowed to touch them. I had to learn to keep my hands to myself. I wanted to be careful of what I was doing at school.

When I had a bad day at Thurgood Marshall, I yelled, screamed, cried, and threw things at the wall and the window. My old teacher warned me to stop and wanted me to calm down. Whenever I did something bad at school, I got time-outs and was sent home. I was on the school bus and I had a hard time sitting still. I played with the bus windows, the bus driver told me to stop it. During the morning; I tried to wake up and I was still tired. My parents wanted me to get up, but I didn't. Sometimes I felt in pain as I got up. My school bus came on time in the mornings, I heard honking. If I didn't have myself ready, I had to rush myself to get ready. I wasn't in a good mood sometimes while I was on the school bus heading to school. I had meltdowns on the school bus and at the school. My old bus driver told me not to do anything. I said some rude things to my bus driver, every time my old bus drivers got mad at me when I did something wrong that I wasn't suppose to do.

I got frustrated when my old teacher told me what to do. At age five, I started kindergarten at the same school, which is Thurgood Marshall Elementary. I got myself a new teacher with all the new students in a new classroom back then. The students also have Autism too. During class, I was really irritated and frustrated that I couldn't do my schoolwork. When my teacher gave me a hard time, I hit and bite students from my class. I hated to do that, but that's what I felt. My teacher grabbed me and put me in time-out for doing the wrong things. I don't like time-outs that much. It makes me very mad and wanted to yell when I take time-outs. I kicked some light objects and threw everything down on the ground, I was having a meltdown. I was calming myself down after I stopped. I cleaned everything I threw down after I had a meltdown.

Early in the morning, my mom took me to a daycare every day. I was not into daycares that much, it irritated me more often. Sometimes I felt upset about what the people did to me at the daycare. I felt scared that I would get whooped by a daycare person. I got along with my old friends at the daycare. Something I did accidentally to the little babies at the daycare, I took a time-out there also. I always got in trouble at the daycare and at school too. I shouldn't get in trouble, but I did sometimes. I liked to do respectful things while I was at the daycare. After school was out, I went to my school bus and I wanted to sit up front. The problem was… the student took the front seat, the driver wanted me to sit at the back, and I didn't feel like sitting back there. I was yelling and screaming at the bus driver when the bus driver argued with me.

While I was still on the school bus heading back to daycare, I was still really mad at the bus driver. I said something mean and bad to the bus driver. I noticed that the bus driver didn't like it when I talked like that. The bus driver stopped the bus, came back to me, and slams my head back and forth really hard. I started to cry very hard after the bus driver did that to me. The bus driver was mean sometimes, it depends how the bus driver feels. When I was really young I never expected that would happen. We got to daycare, the bus driver told the person from daycare what I did, and I got off the school bus. The person from daycare gave me a time-out for what happened that day.

While I was still at Thurgood Marshall, I had a new speech teacher. I had speech once a week. My old speech teacher helped me with saying words and synonyms. My speech teacher was helping me how to say good things instead of bad. I had to learn what was expected and unexpected. I didn't pay attention that much when I was in class and speech. The speech teacher wanted me to pay attention. It was very important for me to listen to my teacher and parents. Also, I had to say words right so that people would understand me.

Next to Thurgood Marshall Elementary, there's an art center we always went to for Art. I had an old Art teacher who helped me with my project. I like to draw everything and paint pictures. And I wasn't good at sketching when I was young; my old art teacher does sketching. I made crafts on pictures, made a hat, and bracelets for the teachers. I have learned art a lot those years; I usually created stuff. People thought that I'm a good artist. I've seen paintings by famous artists at the Seattle Art Museum. I wanted to be an artist when I grew up. Art was my favorite subject ever! I drew pictures of myself, my friends, and my family.

At my old school Thurgood Marshall, we had gym during one hour. My old gym teacher, her name was Ms. Harvey; she was really nice and beautiful. She usually wanted me to focus on gym class. She was a gym teacher for special Ed. During gym time, we have to climb up the bars. But for me I couldn't. I was afraid of heights that I might fall and get hurt. I didn't want that to happen to me. The bars are twenty feet high; I would never climb that high. So, I climbed high enough, I couldn't go on, and I just went back down. Ms. Harvey said, "Why can't you climb way up to the bars?" And I said, "Because I'm scared and I'm gonna fall." Then, Ms. Harvey said, "Well, you have to climb way up those bars next time, or I will help you climb up to the top." And then, I said, "But I can't do it." Ms. Harvey wouldn't listen to what I was trying to say. When I said something funny to Ms. Harvey, she didn't understand what I was saying. I looked at her shirt and I wanted to see what was inside of her shirt; she didn't want me to touch her. It was inappropriate to touch teachers' clothes, it's called sexual harassment. If that happens, students will get suspended or expelled from school, it depends what kind of trouble it is. I was suspended like two times when I was at Thurgood Marshall. My mom was mad at me when I got in trouble at school.

I had an old music teacher; we went to music on Wednesdays and Fridays. Well, I was into music when I first started listen to it since I was four years old. When I learned how to sing, it felt like I was singing in front of an audience or something. My teacher helped me with the music and taught me how to play a piano. I learned how to play a piano when I was little at my grandmother's house. I was into that as well when I was listening to music. Music is one of my favorite things I like to do in my life. There was a talent show at Thurgood Marshall when I was there. And there was also a music concert as well. I played a piano at the talent show and the music concert. I always like to play a piano some days. Everyone likes to play on pianos when they have great spirits.

When the time came, I had to say good-bye to my old classmates and my old teachers. I was at Thurgood Marshall Elementary School from 1996 to 2002. It was great knowing all the people there that they cared about me. I was very sad that I was leaving my old school, but I would remember it. They served me well, helped me think of my future goals, and they will miss me. For me, I just wanted to stay there, but I had to do what they said. I will miss them as well. I was crying a lot after I left Thurgood Marshall; everything had changed. All the people would remember me when I was there. I was funny and I always like to make people laugh and funny. Also, they liked to tell me jokes.

After I left Thurgood Marshall in Seattle, I got transferred to Renton School District. I went to Lakeridge Elementary School when I was in 4th grade. I got to know all the people there the same way like I did when I went to Thurgood Marshall. But their Autism was different than mine. I always like to talk with people and teachers. I ate lunch with the teachers and the students. When I had learned some skills at Lakeridge, I was ready to go out in a different world. I had a resource teacher as well; her name was Ms. K.J., which stands for Kendall-Johnson. She was really nice and honest, and she helped me with part of my schoolwork. I was out with people in General Ed; I was really shy. But I was getting used to be with regular people. I was always into regular people; I wanted to be regular like everyone else.

It didn't work out for me being at Lakeridge; so I got transferred to another school that was close by where we used to live by Fairwood. I went to Benson Hill Elementary School for a half year. I was really scared of that school because I met too many new people and I was afraid that I would get hurt. I met a new teacher and a new principal at Benson Hill Elementary. It didn't matter if I was scared or not to meet many new people at a new school. I was definitely new there and I took a little tour around the school. I got in trouble there as well, like I did at Thurgood Marshall in Seattle. Well, I'm into girls, but it bothers me when I was trying to focus in school. I got upset when my new teacher didn't help me with my classwork. My aid wasn't around sometimes when I was in class. During lunch at Benson Hill; I started to cry and said, "I want my mommy." I always got lost around a new school when I tried to find someone. That school was too crowded for me to be in. I wasn't into crowds all the time, but sometimes I was into them. I was trying to handle myself, but I got into trouble a lot.

At this moment, I was got into a deep wrath of trouble. I was getting agitated with the other teacher; I terribly grabbed and touched the teacher. I did a really terrible thing; my year didn't work out well. So, I got sent to the principal's office and I felt upset. My aid was very mad at me for what I did, because it was wrong. I just don't know why I did a terrible thing for. People asked me have I lost my mind. I did lose my mind once; but I don't all the time. When it comes to a terrible reputation, I got expelled from Benson Hill Elementary School. I was a bad kid at that school; I won't go back there anyway. At first, I was a good kid when I got to Benson Hill; I got to know all the people, and then at last, it was a blow-out. I had already said good-bye to Benson Hill Elementary; I would remember it too, maybe.

After I got expelled from Benson Hill, I got transferred back to Lakeridge. It was really terrible that I went back at Lakeridge; I would've had stayed at Benson Hill, but they didn't want me there anymore. So, I had to stick with the school that helped me complete until the end of the school year. Since I went back to Lakeridge, I was no longer with the students who had Autism. I was with regular students in General Ed class. We went to gym after recess was over; I liked gym class those years. I got in trouble at Lakeridge too; but I don't like to get in trouble. It happened to me when I was nine years old. I went to detention two times for doing wrong things. During my 5th grade year at Lakeridge, everything was different when I had a new teacher who was teaching with the 5th grade students. We went to field trips as a whole class. Before the last week of school, we all had field day on that final day. The terrible part of my year was that I drew pictures of girls and gave them to my old friends who are girls. My aid didn't appreciate me doing that. That might scare the girls a lot. It depended on how they felt and what kind of girls they are. I went to my 5th grade graduation at Lakeridge Elementary; people that I got to know there would miss me and the 5th graders. Everyone at Lakeridge thinks that I'm a nice and cool person; they would remember of who I am.

That's me in 5th grade at Lakeridge Elementary School

On February 2003, I joined my after school program called Boys and Girls Club at Skyway. Sometimes I do my homework there; but my staff told me to. It's really important for me to do my homework at the club. At Skyway Boys and Girls Club, they have lots of stuff; including game of pool, ping-pong, a pop machine, and teen room. Power Hour is an activity that people spent time on their homework. Our staff served us some goody snacks after Power Hour. Then, we went to the gym at Dimmitt Middle School to play around during that time. Ms. Dorina, one of the staff, knows I done good to receive my goals. All of the staff at Boys and Girls Club are so awesome and good when I was there. We took field trips on the Boys and Girls Club van to everywhere we go. We went to another Boys and Girls Club at Kirkland; it was really fun when we play games, eat food, and watch the video that they made there. Also, we went to Fisher Plaza to watch Northwest Afternoon in 2005.

When my year came, I went to Dimmitt Middle School for 6th grade. It was really different when I first experienced middle school. I saw my same friends; but I met other new people there as well. When I first came to Dimmitt, I saw my aid and he was going to be with me that year. I had six classes with all the teachers; I was very shy. Dimmitt Middle School has lockers and other portables. This was my first time that I had a locker in middle school. While I was at Dimmitt, I was talking to girls, and to everyone else. But I had to keep it simple; I really wanted to focus on education. I got in trouble at Dimmitt all the sudden because I hit girls and other boys. I really don't like hitting people; but that's what I felt like doing when the students didn't talk to me. When I said hi to people at Dimmitt, sometimes they ignored me. I really don't like to be ignored by students and others. I said hi to the girls in the hallway; I scared them away and I don't know why I did that. I think I made the girls uncomfortable when I talked to them that way. I don't like to scare people; but they say I always do. I couldn't believe that people were saying those kinds of things; I just wanted to be friendly and seem calm to others.

That's me in 6th grade at Dimmitt Middle School's Book Fair on May 12th, 2005

I got homework from some of my classes; I didn't do any of it. I don't know why they gave me lots of homework; it made me really frustrated. I got good grades when I did my classwork; I really don't like getting bad grades. It was extremely important for me to do my studies. People did not do their studies that often; they wanted to go out with friends. I didn't go out with friends until I finished my homework though. If I had a messy room; I cleaned up my room, but not all the time. My parents would tell me to clean up my room before I did anything. My room was always messy and I wanted to keep it clean. I made a mess sometimes, but I don't like to make messes. While I was at lunch, I ate my lunch too fast and I couldn't slow down. I always wanted to be careful with the way I ate. While I was in class, I had to listen what the teacher was talking about. Every time I felt tired and my aid told me to sit up, because I got too much energy and had trouble sleeping. When I didn't listen, my aid told me to listen to the teacher talking. Whenever I felt upset in class; I just walked out of the classroom and my aid followed me and said, "Alex, what's wrong? I want you to stop walking right now." And I would say, "I don't want to talk, leave me alone!" I sat down by the wall and I was crying a little. I didn't realize that it was really hard for me to go to all my class every day. My aid told me it was gonna be hard for me and it would go on forever. I wouldn't know until it came.

During my 7th grade year at Dimmitt; it was my worse year, because I got in trouble a lot, too much trouble that I was tried to deal with. I was always hitting girls. I failed two classes, Science and World History; I felt upset that they didn't help me pass my classes. It got worse and some of my friends stopped talking to me and told me something rude. They all made me angry and I wanted to hit them. But I really didn't want to hit them that much; it would get me into a lot of trouble if I kept doing that. Some of my friends told me that people called me a retard. It was not nice that they were saying about me. Others made fun of me at Dimmitt and I don't like to be made fun of. While I was in the bathroom, I felt agitated, I yelled at myself and hit myself. I banged my head in the bathroom wall as I said terrible things. I couldn't control myself and I really wanted to calm down. I apologized to all the girls I had hit and they said that they forgave me. Since I hit a lot of people at Dimmitt, I got suspended lots of times and I lost my privilege to go to class before the class bell rang. I had to go to class after the second bell rang. I wanted to complete and pass all of my classes before the school was out for the summer. I had my privilege back during the last day of school. I said good-bye to everyone at Dimmitt; I took pictures of them with my disposable camera, and spent my summer off from school. During the summer, I went to the school camp called Camp Walkapala. I went there from July to August 2004 and July to August 2005. I went there for both summers and it was very fun!

In 2006, I started the organization called Boys in Action. It is part of the YMCA group and I like it a lot. After school, Boys in Action took place at my old school which is Dimmitt Middle School. My old friend and I used to go there every Wednesday. We did something fun at the YMCA Boys in Action. We went bowling at the Fairwood bowling alley; we had so much fun there. Our Boys in Action counselor, Joseph, was one of the greatest staff that I remembered when I first came to that program. I love being part of the YMCA Boys in Action group. It was a very fun and great program to be in when we did all kinds of great stuff!

That's me and my old friend by Dimmitt Middle School for YMCA
Boys in Action in the summer of 2006

That's me when I was at Subway with my classmates from
Eckstein Middle School

On beginning of September 2006, I found out that I was no longer going to Dimmitt, because my aid became a teacher at Renton High School and I got signed back to Seattle School District when we moved back to Seattle. I felt sad that I wouldn't be at Dimmitt anymore. I was gonna miss my old friends at Dimmitt and they will remember me for how nice I was. For one day, I went to Hamilton International Middle School with my sister. After that, I got transferred to another school because Hamilton didn't have the program I needed to be in. I found a school that was right for me; Eckstein Middle School. I went there for 8th grade; I met new people and new teachers. My brother and my cousin went there a long time ago. Eckstein was a great school to go to for great education. Suddenly, I was talking to girls at Eckstein and introduce myself to them. But my new aid told me that I shouldn't talk to girls. Every time I got frustrated, I kicked the wall and the desks in portable 8, which was our classroom. All the teachers made me mad, because I had to do my homework and classwork. I took deep breaths and wanted to be alone. I talked with my counselor who helped me express my feelings. I got suspended from there also because I got in trouble with two girls who were my friends. I really didn't like to get in trouble at Eckstein either. I wanted them to respect me and I would respect them.

While I was at Eckstein, I learned new things from my new classes. There were seven periods every day, which was new for me. During lunch, I went to the room called the Game Room. I played a video dance game called DDR, which stands for Dance Dance Revolution. The days I didn't go to the Game Room, I went to Portable 7 to eat my lunch. The students and I watched a movie during lunch every day. I always like to do all those things while I was still at Eckstein. When I've completed all of my work, I felt worn out after I got all of my classes done. When the time came, I graduated from Eckstein Middle School and I was going to miss being there. My teachers and all of my friends will miss me a lot; they will remember me. I started to go to summer school at Ballard High School during the summer, after I graduated from Eckstein.

Chapter Three
My Teenage Years

After my childhood ended, I've became a teenager at age 13. It was a new generation and my life. I have to do the best I can to be respectful to others. I get to the point that I talk badly to others and hurt their feelings. I had to be careful of what I did and didn't get into more trouble. It made me want to move out. I wasn't ready for that; I had to live under my parents rules.

On October 2006, I hung out with my old best friend named Dana. Dana and I went to school together at Eckstein. I went to the pumpkin patch with him and his family. It was pretty fun to go. We looked at the pumpkins and rode on the pumpkin truck. When we got back from the pumpkin patch, I hung out with him at his house until my mom was on her way to pick me up. Ben had a dog named Irish, which is a good name for a dog. His dog was shorter like a leprechaun. He and I were watching the British comedy show called Blackadder; it was a funny show to watch, it was made way back in the 80's. After that, his mom called us for dinner, so I joined him and his family for a nightly dinner. While I was eating dinner with them, my mom just came to pick me up. My mom met my best friend and his dad when she dropped me off. I really had a fun time hanging out with my friend Dana. Dana also has Autism like me; he walked from Eckstein to his house after school, I saw him when I was on the school bus.

That's me when I was between 13 and 14 years old and still in my last year in middle school.

When I was at my grandmother's house visiting my grandmother, I felt down because I got suspended from Eckstein Middle School for writing a threatening note to my teacher, which I shouldn't have done. It all started when I was in my 7th period class in Washington State History. I tried to do my classwork, my special ed. teacher told me to look on the board; but I knew what I was doing. The teachers and aides wouldn't believe me; they told me to do my work, which made me frustrated. When class was over, I wrote a bad note for my special ed. teacher, which was terrible. I gave the note to my teacher and I ran out of the classroom as I went out for my school bus. In the next morning I came to school, my administrator, Mr. Kingsley, wanted me to come to his office. He found out what I did, he was not happy that I wrote a bad note to Ms. Phelps, which is my special ed. teacher. I told my cousin what happened at school that day; he was a little disappointed in me and wanted me not to do it anymore. Then, he let me go and I talked to my other cousin about what happened as well at his room. After I told him; he told me that I wrote a bad note to my teacher because I didn't want to talk to her anymore; he wanted me to apologize to my teacher and he hugged me. I was crying and he helped me how to solve my problem. I went back upstairs and apologized to my uncle; then he hugged me too. Afterwards, I apologized to Ms. Phelps for writing a bad note and she forgave me.

At age 14, during the summer, I started the program called Special Olympics. I first started to join Special Olympics at age 12 for cycling. That year, I did softball with the students with disabilities. I like doing softball, it's like a baseball, and I like baseball. Every Monday and Thursday I went to Renton High School to do the baseball practice for the Special Olympics tournament. At the first tournament, we had to get ourselves ready for the game. My coach wanted our team to win the gold medal. During the game, the players took turns and went to their positions. We did the game well, but we lost in the first baseball tournament. There was another event tournament that came up on that same day. We have to do more practice on baseball, so we can get better at it. At the second tournament, it was a final moment for playing the Special Olympics baseball game. It will be the last time playing baseball and the season would end. We got in to our positions and beat the team. Then at the end of the second tournament, we did it, we won the game! We won a gold medal and I felt really happy about it.

On October 2007, my mom packed up my stuff for me and sent me to a hospital home called Fairfax Hospital. I wasn't expected to be at a home. I thought I was there for a check-up; but they told me it was a home. I wasn't into hospital homes at all. I was really mad at myself at the moment; I didn't want to be there right now. I was spending time at Fairfax with some new people from my age group. I missed living at home; I wanted to go trick or treating on the other day. But I had to stay there until the time they let me out; we all went trick-or-treating on people's doors at Fairfax. It was fun, but not all the way. When that time came; it was time for me to leave Fairfax as my mom came to pick me up.

On January 2008, I went out with my mom somewhere and I was hungry. I asked my mom if she could take me to Burger King; I got the Burger King coupons, but my mom said she wouldn't take me there. My mom said she had food at the house; I didn't eat the food from home that often. I really wanted to go to burger king badly; but still my mom didn't take me there. I was getting a little irritated and I was eating the donuts I bought; but my mom didn't want me to eat all the donuts. My mom wanted me to give her the donuts; I got very upset and angry with my mom. My mom stopped the car at the same spot where I was run away as a little kid. She doesn't appreciate me talking to her like that. I hit my mom again as I kept talking bad to her. My mom couldn't take it anymore, so she called the police, I told her I didn't mean to and didn't know what was wrong with me, but she couldn't handle it. She was very upset with me when I hit her a few times and talked to her like that while we were in the car. I got really explosive, stepped out of the car, and slammed the door. My mom was not safe with me and she told me that I needed some help; I was getting really agitated. I told my mom I promised that I wouldn't do it anymore; but my mom couldn't help me and she was scared of me. While she was on the phone talking with the emergency, I told my mom that I was sorry; she said that I was not sorry. Then, it got me all frustrated and angry, I came to hug her; she didn't want me near her right now. So, I grabbed her and slammed her back at the car. She said when she was crying, "Alex, why did you do that? How could you?" I was crying really hard and I ran away from her when I went by my old school, Thurgood Marshall Elementary. After I got back, the police, the firefighters, and the emergency van had arrived, they took me away to Harborview; I was crying a lot when I got there. At night-time, I left Harborview and got sent back to Fairfax, which was a terrible thing. I wouldn't have done a bad thing to my mom; I don't like to be mean to my family. I can't handle myself, that's why. After I spent a week at Fairfax, my mom came to pick me up and I apologized to her. I learned that I haven't been taking my pill that is why I was bad when I was with my mom. I called my family members like my aunt and another cousin. I told my aunt that I was okay and she was happy. I also told another cousin that I was okay, but he was really upset with me.

After that day, I got in trouble at school with the boy in my drama class; I went with my aunt to go see my grandmother at her house during January 2008. Another cousin was there and wanted me to have a talk. My cousin and I went downstairs to his room; the other cousin moved out of there months ago during 2007. When we started our conversation, I was getting to the point that I felt uncomfortable. I went to my grandmother's room and slammed the door. I went on the bed, put my head on the pillow, and started to cry. My grandmother came in to check on me, I was still mad at my cousin at that moment. I needed to be alone for a minute. My mom and my sister just arrived at my grandmother's house, they saw what happened. My mom had a talk with my cousin, which is her oldest nephew. My mom, sister and I were leaving my grandmother's; my cousin apologized to me and I apologized to him as well.

On March 2008, I went to Powell Barnett Park to play around. I like to blow bubbles at every park I go to. All the kids from every park catch the bubbles I blow. While I was at park, I was playing Star Wars with my light sabers by myself. A girl came to me and said, "Hi." I said, "Hi." She asked me if she could play Star Wars with me and I said, "Sure. By the way what's your name?" Then, she said, "Tonika." Then, I said, "Hi Tonika, my name is Alex, nice to meet you." And Tomina said, "Nice to meet you too." I never met a girl who said hi to me before; she was really nice and beautiful. We started to play Star Wars; it was very fun to play that game. After we played Star Wars, I met her mother and her name was Tree. She was nice to me and thought I was a wonderful person. During May 2008, my birthday month; I invited Tonika and her family to my birthday party. My birthday party was at ACME Bowling Alley, while we were there, Tomina and her family showed up. I was so happy that they came to my birthday party. After I went to my summer program, I went to visit Tonika at her house and spend time with her. Tonika and I became best friends when we first met at Powell Barnett Park.

On February 2008, I thought of an idea that I could do for a business. I started to make bracelets and sell them to all the people and kids. That would be my new thing to do for me to keep myself busy. I sold lots of bracelets to the people I knew, they said they were beautiful and nice. I always like to sell bracelets to people and make money. I also sold bracelets when I was at school and at church. Next part is I also made Necklaces; I put them with the bracelets I made. I sold both bracelets and necklaces at the same time. And I also made Beaded Rings, I sold them as well. All of my friends liked the jewelry I made and they bought them from me. I'm a great entrepreneur. Some other people weren't interested in buying my jewelry those days, but it was fine with me. I named my business, Alex's Famous Jewelry in 2010. People I know liked my jewelry the most.

During the months in 2008, I came to visit my neighbor, Charlie, and his wife, Nella, at their house. Charlie is one of my dad's friends, they've been friends for years and they drank beer together. Every time I went to his house, he invited me in and I watched TV with him. It was great that I was spending time with my neighbor, but they didn't want me to come there that often. They would be going out, sick, or sleeping during the day. When Charlie was not around, I came over to his house and his wife was Nella was there. I was also spending time with his wife all the sudden, but not often though. Charlie wanted to spend time with his wife more, but not me. Some of my neighbors had issues and others didn't have issues. Charlie and Nella took me out to dinner with them at the restaurant called XXX. I really like that restaurant, they served big burgers and gigantic burgers, and it made my tummy growl, I wanted to eat those big darn burgers! After that, we were stuffed and full from eating our burgers. I had an extremely great night with my two neighbors; I was sleeping while Nella was driving her van, and Charlie was sleeping too.

At the neighborhood, I met a friend who lives one house away from me. His name is L.G; we got to know each other and became friends. I first met L.G. in 2007; I came over to his house and said hi. He felt miserable that he had no friends to hang out and talk with. So, I helped him and talked with him. We always like to hang out together as great homies. We take metro buses everywhere; we go to many parks, and many other areas. I met his mother before I met him at the bus stop. I told my friend L.G. what happened at school. He felt worried that I would get hurt from bad people.

At age 15, I got trained to take metro everywhere. I know which buses to take from my home, to parks, stores, and other places. I took a metro bus to my program in the summertime, and for the wintertime. My mom was okay with me taking the metro as long as I didn't stay out too long. Metro buses run differently on schedule, sometimes it comes early, and sometimes it comes late. Depending on the traffic, metro buses never come on time. I take metro with my friends and cousins. It's fun to ride on metro to every place. The most important thing is that I can't take metro during the evening; my mom won't like that. I only take metro during the daytime if there was events going on at that time. I like taking metro a lot on these days. Whenever I'm on metro, I seen many of my friends I know and they see me. They are surprised to see me on metro, it makes my day great!

During the summer of 2009, I left my summer job program for the other program. It's called YLF; it stands for Youth Leadership Forum. It's a program for people with disabilities and I enjoyed it a lot. I met new people there, we did some great activities and we had our own dorms. YLF is at Evergreen State College in Olympia; it took at least two and a half hours to get from Seattle to there. We go to breakfast every morning at the college cafeteria; also we get lunch from there as well. We also did riding tricycles around the college and I kinda did rock-climbing; I was still afraid of heights and I might fall down. It was a very interesting program to be in, we watched the magician doing tricks, we did a talent show, and we had a celebration dance before the last day of the program. I like all my friends and staff there; they're very awesome!

That's Bree and me at the YLF classroom, August 2009

In my teenage years, I went to many doctor's appointments. I see my psychiatrist every month when I have problems at school. I went to Swedish Hospital to get my blood drawn out; which is really intense. I wasn't afraid of needles at all, they took my shot, I didn't yell or scream, and I was calm. Then, I went to my dentist appointments. I wasn't afraid to go to the dentist at all either. I brushed my teeth all the time, but sometimes I don't brush my teeth. If I don't brush my teeth, my gums will bleed and cause swelling. The dentist cleans out my teeth and puts in fillings to make my teeth numb. When I have a broken tooth, they put me to sleep, and they take it out. They put gauze on my tooth hole, so it won't get infected.

On April 2010, I took the 106 down to rainier beach and I got off. I took a 7 to Rose St.; I came over this area to see my friend, Elaine Kong. I asked a person if she was home, the person said bad things to me. I don't know why he said that to me. I noticed that those people lived next door to her, are gangs. I heard about what gangs are. I was a victim of those gangs at rainier beach. They don't know that I have Autism, but they don't believe that. I said some rude things to the gangs, I ran away from them as they ran after me. I got myself in danger with those gangs and they wanted me to go. The gangs scared me away and I called the police on them. When the police arrived, I told them what was going on. People who lived in the area told me not come there anymore; it was not safe for me to go to that area where the gangs are.

I already noticed that I shouldn't be stalking people at their homes. It's a bad thing to stalk people at their homes. When I have friends who I go to school with, they don't give me their numbers. So, I look them up online and see where they live, I know it's a really bad thing to do. Some of my friends give me their numbers and addresses, they're okay with that. When I came to a friend's house, my friend told me that she or he didn't expect me to come. They told me to leave and I was mad at myself, I should move on with better friends. They said that they could call the police on whoever stalks in front of their houses. I shouldn't be stalking friends' houses unless they expect me with a purpose. When I come over to my other friend's house, I told a parent that I'm one of their friends who went to school with them; they will get my friend and bring him or her to me. My friend was surprised that I came over to his/her house. I had to ask my friends first before they expect me to come at their house. Stalking is a terrible thing that I shouldn't think about.

During the summer in my teenage years, I still have a Kool-Aid stand. When summer comes, I add Lemonade with my stand. Now it's called Lemonade and Kool-Aid stand. A lot of people are into Lemonade these days, when it's really hot out. Some of my neighbors came to my stand many times during the summer. They think that I'm a great business person and I make great tasting lemonade. I noticed that I was getting too old to do the Lemonade and Kool-Aid stand. But people like my stand the most and they want me to keep on doing it. Every summer I do the stand and all the kids want to buy Lemonade and Kool-Aid from me. I make lots of money from doing the Lemonade and Kool-Aid stand. I will remember it in my head and in my good memories. People will miss having my Lemonade and Kool-Aid stand. They will remember me as the one best person who did the stand every summer.

Sometimes I ask my friends who are girls, what size shoes they're wearing. They tell me their size and ask me why I'm asking. I tell them I'm just asking. I bought them sandals as a gift. I told the girls I bought them gifts, they were surprised and they said, "You shouldn't have done that, Alex. But that was very nice of you though." I said, "I always have to do that, I just want to make you girls happy, and you all are my very nice and beautiful friends!" And they said, "Aww thanks Alex. You're so sweet!" When I gave them their gifts, they open them, and they noticed that those sandals are cute. Some of the girls hug me when I give them gifts. But I shouldn't spend my money on people like that. They won't appreciate me buying them gifts and never accept them. I have to be careful what I spend my money on, that will get me into deep trouble. I have taught myself that I shouldn't buy gifts to people anymore. It will make them upset when I buy them gifts. I only buy gifts if people's birthdays are coming up. I feel bad when I spend money on people's gifts. I've already learned my lesson from it.

All the time I always listen to my favorite songs and they make me want to sing them. I like to listen to old school music; it's my favorite era that I like. I'm into that kind of music. I made up a stage name for myself; I was into hip hop/rap. My old stage name was D.T. Cartell and my new stage name is Fantasy A. People think that I rap very well and my friends also think that my songs are tight. I give them great spirits with my rap career. I started to do rap at age 14; I have had some more practice. Sometimes I mess up saying the words when I write a rap song. It's really hard to memorize the song in my head. I took my time to get it memorized and I would get good at it. I have a good memory, but sometimes I have a bad memory. Everyone I know likes my songs that I write; it makes them happy and excited. Whenever I feel frustrated and angry, I write a song about how I feel. It was really important for me to write something about my feelings.

I joined the site called Facebook, it's an okay site, but you can tell if you put bad feelings on there, people will see it. Facebook is not a safe site to put my terrible things on; it will get me into a lot of trouble. I really don't want to get in trouble on the site. I have friends on Facebook and I try to get other people to add me, but they don't accept me as a friend. It makes me upset and angry if people don't accept me and write back to me. That one time, I put up a bad status about my friends that was terrible. When they saw that, they were hurt, I hurt their feelings. I really don't like to harass people on Facebook that will get into my criminal records; I don't want that to happen. I wanted to be friendly and good to people on Facebook. I put up a good status about my friends and my day. My friends would like that when they see it. I kept in touch with them and they kept in touch with me. If I hurt their feelings, they want me to give them space. After days pass, I apologize to my friends about what I said on Facebook. The problem was before that I talked to girls I like on Facebook, sometimes they didn't want to be bothered, I was trying to get in contact with them, and they never responded to me. It got me worried that they were talking to someone else instead of me. So, I said some mean things to the girls I used to like and they deleted me off from their friend list. I only write messages once a while when my friends are ready for it. It's good that I gave them time to take a break from Facebook. I would take a break from it too.

I was tired of my parents making me angry when I did something around the house. On April 18th, 2010, while I was at home with my dad that night, we were planning to go out for dinner at Applebee's. I felt better when I stopped crying. We went out to Applebee's for dinner and that made us happy again!

Chapter Four
My High School Years

After I graduated from middle school months ago, I started a new life in high school. The school I went to is called Cleveland High School. I heard it used to be in the West Seattle neighborhood; and then they remodeled Cleveland back to Beacon Hill. Everything changes when people go to high school. I was shy when I first experienced high school. I started to go to Cleveland in my freshman year; I saw some of my old friends that went to Thurgood Marshall with me years ago. I met many new people there as well; they thought I was a nice person. High School was hard for me, but I was getting used to it. I met some new teachers and had new classes at Cleveland High School. I like all of the people I met, they were so nice and cool, and they like me. I had lunch with my teacher and the students, it was good. I took a tour around at Cleveland, it has three buildings, and it's a big school.

While I was at Cleveland, I made some friends and I always liked to talk with them. There are three people who I've met at Cleveland who are my homies. I met Ricardo and Angel. I saw them every single day when I was at Cleveland. Then, I met a guy named David; he's the coolest person ever! In my sophomore year at Cleveland during the last day of school, I met two of the nicest people who signed my yearbook, Jose, and the nicest, the one, the only girl I always like and think about in life, Ximena a.k.a. Mina Angel. Some of those people made my day great and incredible those days. I am really happy and excited that they're being my good, awesome, and amazing best friends and homies. They always think that I'm a cool and awesome person.

Every time I was in high school at Cleveland, I was into talking to all girls I liked there. Some of the girls weren't interested of me and won't talk to me. I always like talking to girls a lot, but I shouldn't talk with them if they're not interested of me. All other girls like me when I talk friendly and respectfully. Sometimes when I didn't talk right, I scared the girls away and I wanted to talk to them. Some girls felt uncomfortable of the way I talked to them, I had to talk gently to them. I was saying something to the girls in the hallway at Cleveland, but I followed them. It made them uncomfortable when I and others followed the girls, I shouldn't have followed the girls. I just want to get the girls to like me that was why I was trying to get their

That's me with and my friends, Mina and Jose at my neighborhood Skyway on May 2011

attention. Because of my autism, other girls aren't interested in me. I got in trouble by hitting girls I like and writing them bad notes. Some of the friends I know treated me badly and the other friends I also know treated me nicely. I got suspended a lot for doing bad things at Cleveland High School. People can't handle me that much when I do terrible things.

During lunch, I was outside with my classmates and all the students were outside as well. After I met two girls, the other girl called out and she said, "Would you like some Candi?" I said, "Yeah, I like some candy." She said, "It ends with an I." I didn't notice the word ended with an I that was really weird. She asked me to put my hand together with her hand; she had lots of bracelets on her right arm. While we had our hands together, she slid one of her bracelets off her arm and right through my wrist. She called her bracelets Candi and her nickname was Sparkles. But her name is Jennifer; she was a beautiful and nice person. We hung out during lunch and we talked together. After the bell rang when lunch was over, she told me that I forget to kiss her on the lips. So, I kissed her on the lips that told me that Jennifer and I were in a serious relationship. I was a freshman and she was a sophomore when we first met, and we added each other on MySpace. I tried to reach Jennifer over the summer in 2008, she didn't answered. When months had passed when school started again, I was a sophomore and Jennifer was a junior. I found that she told me that she had a boyfriend. She already broke my heart and I felt bad about her. I was trying to win Jennifer back and not let her be with that other boy, but it didn't work. On March 2009, when that time came, I wrote a message to Jennifer on MySpace and she said when she wrote me back, "Alex, it will be in my interest if you stopped talking to me. Thanks." It made me sad and she hurt my feelings. Jennifer wasn't nice to me at all, well I was thinking about her too much and I gave her too much stuff. That was why Jennifer wanted me to not talk to her. About thirteen days before the last day of school, Jennifer still didn't want me to talk to her, I wrote her a bad message and she wrote a rude message back to me. So, I didn't talk to Jennifer anymore after what she did to me, it was very bad to me. We don't deserve each other after all.

My teacher planned on having field trips for me and the students. While we were out of Cleveland, we went out of the community. Mondays, we went swimming and grocery shopping, Thursdays, we went bowling which was so fun, and Fridays, we went everywhere around the areas. I always like to go on field trips everywhere. My substitute teacher also took us out into the community every single Friday; I really like the substitute teacher. My teacher told me that I couldn't go with them where they were going, because my teacher said I had to be in my classes. Sometimes I felt frustrated when I didn't do well in my classes; I don't like to fail all of my classes. I was getting used to it and focused on my studies. Whenever my teacher needed me to come with them on field trips, I took my time-off from my classes. I like going on field trips with the students at Cleveland High School.

During my freshman year at Cleveland High School, I was running for school vice-president. Many students were running for their positions on student class elections. I wrote my own speech to say to the students when I was running for vice president. During lunch, they announced the student elections. They called out my name; I got elected as freshman vice president. I felt proud of myself that I became a vice president of the freshman class. People were so proud of me as well and they clapped. I loved being a freshman vice president and I went to student meetings.

All the teachers I had at Cleveland made me very mad all of the sudden. I don't like to be mean to my teachers, but they made me feel this way. My teachers were nice to me all the time, but it got to the point that they were mean to me if I didn't do my work. My aides got mad at me for doing something that I shouldn't do. It got me mad when they told me what to do. It made me hit one of my aides and I got myself in trouble for that. Every time I was at Cleveland I got in trouble a lot, because I did something bad to people. I hate getting mad with people, but they make me mad. I got in trouble by writing a threatening note to my aide, my aide didn't appreciate that. I hit two of the students in my teacher's classroom and I hit one of the students in my other teacher's classroom. I really got into deep trouble when I was at Cleveland. I don't like Cleveland, not that much anymore.

On October 2008, I was running for homecoming duke for the homecoming court. There was a homecoming dance on that exact year; people were running for homecoming court. I also put up flyers, so the students would vote for me for homecoming duke. I was waiting patiently when that time came. I went to Cleveland's football game at the Memorial Stadium in Seattle Center. During the half-time of the game, they announced the students for homecoming court. When that moment came, I got voted as a homecoming duke fore homecoming court. I went to the homecoming dance with my cousin. I like to dance with everybody I know and they dance with me. I was very happy that I became homecoming duke for homecoming court and homecoming dance.

On June 2nd, 2009, I practiced doing the talent show at Cleveland High School. I rapped a song called "Freaks Come out at Night" by Whodini; it was my favorite song to listen to. Everyone was rehearsing for the talent show as well. I went to the talent show that evening to do my favorite song. I thought I did well, but I still participated in the talent show. People applauded to all of us for doing the talent show. I like talent shows and I enjoyed being in them. Everyone enjoyed being in talent shows as well, but they were shy of the audience. I was nervous when I started doing the talent show, but I got used to it. I have great talents and people have good talents as well.

In my junior year at Cleveland, I was running for the homecoming court again. At that time, I was running for homecoming prince. I tried to put up as many flyers as I could, but I didn't have enough. When they announced for homecoming prince for the homecoming court, it was another person who got voted for homecoming prince. So, I lost for homecoming prince, but I was fine with that. I went to the homecoming game at the Memorial Stadium in Seattle Center to watch the game. Sometimes Cleveland loses during the game scores; they wanted to get better at it. After the homecoming game, I went to the homecoming dance by Olympic Room at Seattle Center. I hung out and danced for a little bit until it was time for me to leave. My friend girl and I went to get our picture taken for homecoming. I had a great time at the homecoming dance, I enjoyed it a lot.

On October 26th, 2009, that day was a terrible day. During that morning, I felt down about that Jennifer thing, it still bothered me. After I went to two of my classes, I went to my third period class during passing period. I told my third period teacher that I would be back when my teacher thought I was going to the bathroom. I walked by the stairs and I saw Jennifer walking up the stairs. So, I went behind the wall as Jennifer was going to class, I went towards her, hit her and slam her by the emergency door as I said, "You dumb motherf@#*er!" Jennifer said, "What the f@#* is your problem, Alex?" I walked away from Jennifer and told her to shut up. I went to my new teacher's classroom; I felt angry and upset at that moment; I threw a chair at the wall and I kicked the table. My teacher told me to calm down, so I sat down and I told them what happened. Jennifer was hurt and crying when I did that to her, I shouldn't have done that and I didn't know what was wrong with me. My mom came to school and she was not happy with me of what I did to Jennifer. I was suspended for five days after I did something bad to Jennifer. On November 2009, I got sent to court for an incident of Jennifer from Cleveland High School. Jennifer's dad was at court on that day, he was worried about what I did to his daughter. After court, I had a talk with Jennifer's dad. I felt scared of what I did to Jennifer, which is really shocked. I can't go wander the school because of the problem with Jennifer. I felt frustrated that I couldn't go anywhere I wanted when I was at Cleveland. Jennifer put a restraining order against me, so I could never be that close to her. I would never want talk and contact Jennifer again.

During my terrible junior year at Cleveland, I felt really frustrated that I couldn't go around the school during lunch. I had to stay in my teacher's classroom for lunch. I used to eat lunch at the cafeteria. I couldn't handle myself when I was with my teacher. I got frustrated when I didn't like being at Cleveland High School. I got in trouble too many times there anyway. I stopped going to Cleveland and stayed home for days. I was not planning on going back to Cleveland ever again. My mom took me to the school district in Seattle and told them what was going on. They were thinking about transfer me to another school. When I went back to Cleveland, it was my last day being there when I finished up my classes. I said good-bye to all of my friends and teachers, they would miss me. It was great knowing them at Cleveland High School; people would remember me as a nice and cool person when I was first came to Cleveland. I left the school at the end of December 2009.

On January 2010, I started half of my junior year at the new school in Seattle Center called The Center School. It's an alternative high school that is different than other regular high schools. I took a tour around Center School and saw what it was like being there. I met my new teacher and new aides; they were nice when I was there. There were no school buses that took people to a city school. I felt very happy being at Center School. I got to know all of the new people and new teachers there; they got to know me as well. It was very weird that the people at The Center School are colored and mixed, but I really like that though. I felt really shy of being at a new school, but I was getting used to it. I took a town car from home to Center School, and after school, from there to home. I really enjoyed being at Center School and meeting new people, I missed Cleveland, but I don't like Cleveland anyways.

While I was at Center School, I was into talking with girls a lot of times. It gets to the point that they felt uncomfortable with me talking to them a lot. But, some of the girls like me as a nice friend. Some of the guys I met at The Center School, they think that I'm a cool person and a great ladies man. I just didn't know when they first told me about it. I was trying to keep on walking to class, but I stopped to say hi to the girls; my teacher told me to keep on walking. I really like talking with people when they make me have good days. I was really focused in class when the teacher was talking to the class. The whole class welcomed me to their classroom; I felt really excited about that. They were being respectful and nice to me; they won't be rude to me. I got along with the students at The Center School; it really got me going well.

At the beginning of my senior year at The Center School, I made some Oreo cupcakes to all the students and teachers. That year was an exciting year that all the seniors would be graduating. I was working on my senior project, it was about stenciling. Stenciling was my favorite thing to do; but it doesn't interest me sometimes. I would never get my senior project done at that amount of time, I just forget about that. It was really hard for me to get all of my classes done before graduating. Some of my friends helped me with part of my work; I appreciated them. My teacher was on maternity leave because my teacher was having a baby. My new teacher was very cool and nice; his name was Mr. Massie. He knew that I was a cool guy and a great student. Mr. Massie helped me to get my work done before the school year ended. When I finished all of the classes, it was time for me to graduate. Me and the class of 2011, are cheering around the school and saying, "ONE ONE!" On June 16th, 2011, the time has already come, I graduated from The Center School and I felt very glad that I finished high school.

I started to go to my internship, it's called XIP, and it stands for Exploratory Internship Program. I worked at XIP mailroom on September 2010. I sorted and bundled the mail into the right places, sometimes we made mistakes. I looked on the cover sheets before I put them on the mail. After that, I moved on to delivering mail to the district offices. When I finished delivering mail, I put mail bags for the school mail bags. I did really well on those job activities when my teacher felt proud of me. On September 2011, I started on XIP again; I worked at the place called the STAR Center. It's a place that has a computer lab for people with disabilities. I learned new skills on computers and got good at it. On February 2012, I started to work at another place called SHAG Terrace. It's a place that has housing for seniors. I taught the seniors how to use new computers there. After I departed from SHAG, I got transferred back to STAR Center. I worked as a receptionist at the front desk at STAR Center. I always like to go to XIP; it's a great internship site.

On March 2008, I started to go to an after school program called the TAT program. TAT stands for The Able Teens. I liked working for TAT, it was really hard for me, but I was getting used to it. It's at Jefferson Community Center; it has great people and staff there. On Wednesdays, I started to go to Cultural Kitchen Club at Van Asselt Community Center. I learned how to cook at that program; it took me time to get good at it. I saw my same friends that I went to Cleveland with at the same two programs. I really like TAT and Cultural Kitchen on those days, but I got tired after I quit. I've remembered I used to do TAT and Cultural Kitchen all of the sudden, people would remember me then. During the summer, I started doing the summer job called the STEP program. I worked in this program on July 'til August 2008, 2009, 2010, and 2011. STEP stands for Student Teen Employment Preparation. In 2008, it was at Rainier Community Center for doing Emergency Preparedness, in 2009, it was at Maplewood in Lucille St. for Landscaping, in 2010, it was at Pratt Park for summer camp, and in 2011, it was at South Park Community Center for helping around the community. People would remember me how great at working with them, together as a great team.

On September 2011, I got sent back to The Center School to do the credits I missed. I wasn't expecting that to happen. I saw my friends again and they were so glad that I spent a year with them. I thought I graduated, but I didn't, they told me that I have to finish up those two missing classes. That was very hard to get my credits turned in. Sometimes I got very angry when my teacher sent me back there and I had to do my work. There was construction at The Center House while I was at the school. I had to get my work done as quickly as possible before I moved on. I was talking to three of my friends about everything. I told the girl named Lenna that she had a nice shirt and she said, "Oh thank you." I asked her an inappropriate question, which wasn't really good. I got sent to the principal's office and the principal asked and told me what happened. It was a sexual harassment when I ask girls inappropriate questions. I felt terrible and upset that happened.

After the situation at The Center School, I had a talk with my teacher and my aide about what happened that day. I felt scared of telling them all the stuff I had done. After two days of being at school, I had done another terrible thing. I put up videos on Facebook for the girls I know to see. I had my principal on my Facebook friend list, Ms. Davidova is the name of the principal at The Center School. She saw everything I put up on Facebook; that she didn't feel comfortable with. My mom called me and told me that my teacher just called her about what I did it was wrong. So, I put up a terrible status about myself ending my life. I shouldn't have put it up there, all the people from Facebook would see it, but I did anyways. My mom called me to see if I was okay and I told her I was okay. I told my mom to tell Ms. Davidova that I won't come to school for two days, I needed my time-off from Center School. I got suspended there as well for one time; I really can't believe that happened. I did great things when I was at Center, I shouldn't have ever did something bad there. People from Center School like me and they wanted me to live. While I was not at school, I didn't do anything fun, I just went somewhere and was alone. They found out that I bought girls shoes as gifts; I got in trouble for doing that. My mom and I went to visit Center School to have a personal meeting with my teacher, my district counselor, and my principal. They already knew what I did was wrong. They warned me if I did that again, I would get suspended again which I didn't want. They told me that I had to keep and finish up my academics, which was my goal.

When it was my first day back at Center School, my transportation time was changed. I used to come at school early, but not anymore. I had to be at school when class was starting or after it was started. I had no problem of being late. It was that I couldn't wander around the school anymore because I got in trouble for talking to girls on Facebook and during passing period at school. I had to finish up my classes and keep myself focused. People were asking about me while I was still in the classroom. My teacher told me that my last day of being at Center School was on June 15th. I couldn't wait until that time came to be finished with everything. I felt extremely excited that I got all of my classes done. On June 15th, the time had come to a happy ending of my high school years. I had finished, completed my credits for my two missing classes, I felt amazed. Then, I said good-bye to all of my friends I've known for years at Center. They will miss me and I will miss them as well forever. But, they wanted me to visit them sometime next year. I felt glad that I finally finished high school. People will remember me of how cool I am when I was at Center School.

Chapter Five
Young Adulthood

After I turned 18, I still a teenager, but a young adult. There's a law if I break the rules, I'll be convicted and sent to jail. I don't want to go to jail and do bad things. On June 2011, I was in Downtown Seattle walking around to check on the shops. I went to BECU to get some money out of the machine; I was making sure that anyone wasn't watching me. After I left the bank, the lady came to me and said, "Hi." And I said, "Hi." I don't think that I recognize this lady before; she look just like the people I knew. She asked me if I want to help her; I don't know if I will trust her or not. I told her no thank you; but she didn't listen what I'm saying. She begged me to help her; I decided to do what she said. The lady wrote me a check to take money out for her; she wanted me to go in the bank and do it. I felt uncomfortable about what I was doing. I looked at the person's name on the check; I noticed that the lady stole this person's checkbook. Well, I deposited that check when the lady was watching me; but I should've taken that to the bank clerk to see if this check is good or not. Suddenly, I didn't do it. I took the money out of my account and gave it to the lady. She asked me a random question; I told her my answer. The lady wanted me to go out with her; but I told her no thanks and she's not my age. She said she's my age, I don't believe her. I knew that the lady was lying to me; she begged me to go out with her. I got uncomfortable with her when she talked weird. After that, she left and I ran away. I called the police and made a report. I was a victim like my grandfather; I happened to him as well. I go to the park and I sat on the swing; I felt upset and scared about what happened. I called my grandmother, my older brother, and my mom about what happened with me. They got worried about me and I don't feel like talking.

I thought about doing the lottery; it was an easy thing to do. But, it was hard for me to win the lottery. I did that many times when I first tried it. I did some lottery games on scratch cards; I scratch off and see if I'm a winner. I lose the lottery when I tried. All the people won the lottery and others didn't. I won the small amount of money; which is okay. Maybe in the future, I will be the one that win the lottery. I thought about going to the casino; but I'm not old enough to go there.

All of my friends thought that I'm lucky of what I'm doing. When I have doctor appointments, I remind my teachers and people at the main office. If I did good things, I earned a reward. I'm lucky for that I did. They wanted to get lucky like me; they have to work on it. I'm lucky when I got my work done fast and I would have my free-time. I won special prizes at the job fair; it was cool. I went to the auditions for Seattle Talent; it was interesting. I like to be lucky whenever I did something special.

I started writing play called School Rich. The book is about the students met the new teacher that gives them money to do the schoolwork. They got caught by these meanest bullies at Morris High School. There is a crazy dark lord that make the students disappeared. A small group of friends take upon themselves to destroy the dark lord. It takes place in The Bronx, New York in the 1980's. School Rich is a fantasy-comedy play that I wrote for everyone to see. I worked on that for two years when I got it done. I did editing on my play after I finished it. I got that published on February 9th, 2012. Everybody thought that my play is interesting and great. I'm gonna write plays forever as my own career.

Whenever I'm still thinking about girls, it made me want to look for a relationship. I thought about girls with all races I like. I'm into white girls, Asian girls, Mexican girls, and sometimes black girls. I'm shy of saying hi to the girls I like. I don't want to be a racist of what kind of girls like the most, but that's how I feel about them all the time. They're not interested of me when I talk bad. I have to be respectful to the girls I want to meet. They don't know me much and they're scared of me. I wanted to be nice with them; it depends how they feel about me. I have to be with a good girl who cares about me; not with a bad girl who doesn't care about me. I get angry if the girl don't like me and want to be my friend. It's important for me that I have to take showers when I get a girlfriend. I feel sad when I don't have to be with. They're some of them everywhere that I would find. When I find a girl that is my type; we gonna get to know each other, be best friends first, and then be together. One day, if I see a girl that got hurt, I will help her and call the ambulance. I have to like a girl if she likes me; it would take time when the girl is ready to come to me.

On June 2012, LG and I went to Cleveland High School's graduation at Memorial Stadium in Seattle Center. I'm supporting my old friends that would graduate this year. I knew them since they first came to Cleveland. They called out the names of the class of 2012; I cheered for them. I remember when I was at Cleveland High School. After the ceremony is over, I come around to congratulate to my old friends for graduating. They said thank you to me; I give them CDs as graduation presents. They were glad that I came to their graduation. Some of my friends who were seniors this year did a great job. LG and I are glad that we enjoyed the graduation for Cleveland High School. I would remember my friends when they were there.

On September 2011, I was at home after I went to school. My older brother called me and wanted to show me and others something. He had a video tape on his hand and he asked, "Did you remember what you guys did ten years ago?" And I said, "Oh yeah! I remember what we did ten years ago. But kinda." When my brother played the tape, I couldn't believe what I saw. It was a video tape that my brother recorded us from ten years ago. I felt shy when I watched that; I shouldn't be looking. My mom and my sister saw it too. I felt embarrassed when I saw a second part about my meltdown. The third part of the video is that I was playing Harry Potter at Alki. This was an old tape that my brother kept for ten years. I enjoyed remember it; but it will bring me silly memories.

Before I go to the library, I went to my old best friend's house. Her name is Katie; I went to Lakeridge Elementary School with her during 4th grade. She is beautiful and nice; I always like to talk with her and her family. Katie and her family go to the bowling league as me, my dad, and my sister. Katie and I had class together in Ms. Chow's classroom; we enjoyed it so much. I missed those days when we were kids. We recognized each other at age 15; she lives in Skyway too up around the corner from me. I was surprised that I have saw Katie again that year. I talked to her sister Carrie, her brother Tommy, her mom, her dad Mike, grandfather Bob, stepbrother Nathan, and stepsister McKayla. They are the nicest people that I want to talk with. The best thing about Katie is that, she likes to talk with people, she talks to me respectfully, and she enjoyed her birthday present I got her. Sometimes I missed Katie, but it's fine with me. I remembered Katie so much when I first met her. I like Katie and her family very much; she's my best friend ever.

My house was messier; I hate living in my messy house. I cleaned up everything around the house; but half of it. I lived in Skyway for 19 years now; my neighborhood wasn't that good anymore. It used to be good when I was young. I want to move out of my neighborhood and move in to my new one. The places I want to live at are, Central District, Capitol Hill, Beacon Hill, Broadway, University District, Queen Anne, West Woodland, Ballard, and Fremont. Those are my favorite places that I always go at. My uncle and my aunt used to live in Ballard. My mom was thinking about living in Eastlake; she wants to set up her own business there. My dream is to become a billionaire, a mayor, a writer, and an actor.

Chapter Six
Things I Always Like to Do

Whenever I was bored, I thought of things to do. I asked my friend and homie LG if he wants to hang out with me. LG is bored as well, so we went out somewhere around the cities. LG and I go to Coulon Park all the time when the sun is out during the summer. I like to go in the water when I feel hot. We go to the Seattle Center Fountain, it is very fun and we like to go to the fountain. I like to think of my own plans when I have nothing to do at home. I help LG have a friend to be with, which is me. We went to Aqua Pura Tower at Capitol Hill; I like to go there a lot. I went to Aqua Pura Tower when I was a young kid. I went to Volunteer Park when I was young as well. My favorite seasons are spring and summer. I always love summer when there are sunny days. LG and I always like to go places.

During the weekend, I called to see if my grandmother was there, which is my dad's mother. I called her every single day when I needed to talk with her. I love my other grandmother so much, I been thinking about her all the time. My grandmother and I talk a lot these days when we're on the phone. I visit my grandmother often when she's at home; she been out and doing a lot of things. My grandmother gets around all the time and she walks a lot. I always like to walk around a lot too, I walk everywhere. I got really tired when I walk to lots of places. I walk everyday when I plan to do something. People walk everyday when they have things going on.

When I was little, I was into playing video games. I played an old Nintendo with the Nintendo games. My favorite video game I played on Nintendo was Mega man, I really liked that game. My other favorite video game was Super Mario Bros. 3, I also liked that game. Whenever I had nothing to do, I played video games every time. I play on the Super Nintendo with the Super Nintendo games. My favorite video games for Super Nintendo are, Super Mario World, Donkey Kong Country, and Super Bonk. I also played on PlayStation, the games I like to play are, Twisted Metal III, Mega man X6, Jet Moto 2, and GT2. My cousin likes to play video games as well; he used to have the Nintendo 64. But, my cousin gave it to me as a present, so I can play on it. All of my friends said they like to play video games, but not often. I usually play video games if I feel like it. Some of the scenes for the video game scare me a bit, but I'll control it. I really love to play video games whenever I have time.

Every single year, I plan on having my own birthday party in different places. At age 9, my birthday party was at Chuck E. Cheese's. It was my favorite place to go to win tickets and eat pizza. At age 14, my birthday party was at ACME Bowl. It was also my favorite place to go bowling and play at the arcade. At age 16, my birthday party was also at my teacher's classroom at Cleveland High School. I remember that I had fun times when I was there. At age 18, my birthday party was at my favorite place I always go to, Family Fun Center. I really love to go to Family Fun Center; it has great games to win tickets. At age 19, I had my own birthday party at Pratt Park. I invited two of my favorite friends to my own birthday party; we had a great time. I like to invite some of my friends to my birthday parties; it was great that they showed up.

I always like to pray to God whenever I feel bad and terrible. I go to church every Sunday sometimes, but it depends on what I have going on. In 2006, I started to go to Freedom Church of Seattle in West Seattle. I was a member at that church for a little while. I always like to greet people and talk with them. I felt blessed when God helps me. If I need help, I talk with my old pastor and all the ministers of the church. I used to be an usher at Freedom, but I stopped. My brother is an usher, he still goes to Freedom. On December 2009, I started to go to another church called Bethel Christian Church in Central District. I felt blessed when I was there with new people I liked and loved. I read the bible sometimes, but I have to read it every day. I talked to my bishop and my evangelist at Bethel about what happened with me. They prayed for me and made me feel better. If I had friends who needed help and are sick, I pray for them and make them feel better. When I make wrong choices, I need to read the bible and pray to the lord. I like to go to church when I don't feel safe with everything.

I always like to go to my favorite park called Gasworks Park. I spent time over there to look at the view and take a few pictures. I go to Alki to walk around and look at the view. I really like to look at the views of Downtown Seattle; it makes me want to live by it. I went to Seattle Aquarium with my classmates and we had a good time going there. I went to the Space Needle with the Teen Social group; I like the Space Needle a lot. I bought myself a Seattle CityPass for wherever I go to have fun. In 8th grade, we were on a cruise for a school celebration. I love it a lot when I was on the cruise. I was dancing on the cruise and one girl danced with me. It was fun; I have great memories of what I did special. I always like to hang around at the north end of Seattle; I went to popular shops. I really like to go to all the parks in the north end. I had great times of traveling around Seattle. During sunny days, I traveled a lot when I was out of school. I like to spend time at all of the community centers; I play basketball and meet new people there.

My favorite greatest baseball players of all time are the Seattle Mariners! I love going to the Seattle Mariners game and I enjoyed watching it. Seattle Mariners play their game at Safeco Field; I had my favorite Seattle Mariner players. My family and I went to Safeco Field to watch the game. When I was little, I got to know the Mariners game when I first heard of it. I went to the Mariners game by myself in the summer of 2010; and with the JCC group in 2011. At Safeco Field, the S.T.E.P. group and I did the activities for the Mariners team. The activities are so interesting and it is very fun to be in them. I really love the Seattle Mariners game very much and I'm going to take my friends and family with me to the game one day in the future.

LG and I were thinking about making our own TV show. We named our show, "The Alex & the Star Show." This show is about special parts that were going on in the world, including a talk show too. We expressed our feelings when we made the show; people say that the show is interesting. We planned on making as many episodes as we could. I played various roles that I made up, so did LG. I like to make videos and put them on YouTube. My homie LG wants to put his videos on YouTube, he has a camcorder, but he didn't use it yet. I put videos on Facebook of what I did on those days. All of my friends like my videos I put up; they enjoy watching them. They think that I'm funny and I make people laugh. I'm into comedy skits and make up funny jokes. That's what I like about making videos and having my own show.

In 2008, I met a girl named Tanela or Tenela; she went to Cleveland High School with me. She is a nice and cool person! We became good close friends and we've been friends for four years. We talk to each other when we see each other. We text each other and see what we've been doing while we were away from each other. I saw her when she first came to Center School. We hung out together as best friends at lunch when we were at Center School. We went to Gasworks Park to hang out and look at the view. I like her as a friend and she likes me too. Tenela and I are the coolest, the best and the close of friends. I remember when I saw Tenela on the bus a few times, it surprised me a bit. We had Poetry together in Mr. Purpleberg's class; I like poetry a lot. She went to the movies with LG and I; we saw the last Harry Potter movie, and had a great time. I am very glad that Tenela has been a great close friend to me.

Alexander (left) and his friend Tenela (right) at Gasworks Park on June 2011

At age 9, I went to the fair called Puyallup Fair. I like to go there a lot. Puyallup Fair is my favorite place to go for fun. It has rides, games, farms, and everything else. I love having fun at fairs; it made me wonder how fantastic it was to be in them. At age 10, I went to Puyallup Fair again with my family. I really like that they made Elephant Ears, it's my favorite type of food. I go to Puyallup Fair every single year to have some fun. Puyallup Fair is in Puyallup, it took like at least 50 minutes to get there. I saw some of my friends at Puyallup Fair those years; it surprises me the most. I like eating stacks of curly fries, krusty pups, scones, and funnel cakes. Those are all the things that I always enjoy!

Whenever I was walking around the neighborhood, I was thinking about hanging out with my friends and homies, Ricardo and Angel at their house. I met them when I went to Cleveland High School with them. They are the coolest buddies ever; I kept them company. I played video games with them and it was really awesome. They were bored when they had nothing to do, so I just stopped by their house for awhile. I met Ricardo and Angel's parents and brothers; they're all nice and honest. Ricardo came to hang out with me and LG somewhere; we went to Fred Meyer and Wal-Mart. When I went to the mall and I finished shopping at Safeway, Ricardo saw me and gave me a ride home. Ricardo and Angel live in the same neighborhood around the corner; they're the best homies that I could ever have. I saw Mina and Jose outside of Ricardo's house; they're also my best homies and friends I could ever have. I saw them somewhere around Southcenter and Seattle as well; it really made my day.

At age 11, I was walking around the neighborhood when I saw those two kids riding their bikes. I said hi to them and they said hi back to me. They're my neighbors who live at the same neighborhood as me. Their names are Jessie and Stephanie; they're the nicest and most excellent people I've ever met in the middle of my childhood. I used to play with them a lot when we were kids at one time. We played around the neighborhood when we were doing funny stuff. Jessie and Stephanie likes to laugh a lot, so do I. When years passed, I saw Jessie every day when I was walking around the neighborhood and everywhere. During those passing years, I haven't seen Stephanie, her sister, and her mom; I don't know what happened and where they were. I asked Jessie where they were; he told me that his mom and Stephanie lived in Mexico. I didn't know that until Jessie told me. On December 2011, after I went somewhere and I came back to the neighborhood, I saw Jesse in front of his house; you can't believe of what Jessie told me who was visiting for the Christmas month. There was someone coming out of the house, it was Stephanie. I was very surprised that she was there. During this summer, I saw Jessie once in awhile and I couldn't believe who came to visit again. It was Stephanie

Alexander won the kick-boxing game set on bingo at Puyallup Fair.

again, I was so surprised and it made my day very great! Jessie and Stephanie are the best and the coolest friends and neighbors that I have been with all of my life and I enjoyed being good with them.

I'm into writing poetry; I always love writing my own poems. I joined a poetry class at Jefferson Community Center in 2010; I really enjoyed it a lot. I went to all the poetry events that year; I really enjoyed it. I heard that there was poetry slam event called Youth Speaks. It's about the point of the poetry that conflicts at ages 13-19. I heard about that in Mr. Purpleberg's poetry class with two guest speakers I know. On January 2012, I joined the Youth Speaks poetry slam event at the Fremont Abbey. I read two of my poems I wrote at the slam event; the second poem I wrote is about love. All the people loved my second poem and thought it was really awesome, sweet, and wonderful. I felt very happy and excited that I made it out of the second round of the slam. I went to the second event at Harambee in Renton, my friend LG did his poem there and he got eliminated. I felt sorry for him; they shouldn't let him go like that. LG got very mad with the people at the slam event; I didn't want that to happen to him. I helped him out to make a better poem to write. I didn't go to the third event at Theater off Jackson by Chinatown. I joined the Youth Speaks writing circle at Youngstown Cultural Arts Center in West Seattle; it happens every Tuesday. I went to a Youth Speaks poetry showcase also at Youngstown; I did read a poem I wrote there. The poem I wrote is called "End of the World… Not Gonna Happen." At that time, there was a last and final event for the Youth Speaks poetry slam also at Youngstown. LG and I signed up and we were in it. I read the same poem as I did at the showcase and LG read his poem I wrote for him. We both got eliminated at the last event, so did the others, but it wasn't a big deal. I am very glad that I joined Youth Speaks; I like it, I enjoyed it a lot.

When I was first came to Center School on January 2010, I heard that the students had their own club called Hip Hop Club. It's a club that talks about everything that inspires Hip Hop. I have friends who were in charge of Hip Hop Club, Sam and Peter. They're extremely cool and excellent and my greatest best friends. When I wrote my own songs, they had a recording studio at The Vera Project. The song I wrote was called "Dance Party," people were into this song and thought it was really interesting. During field day at the Memorial Stadium in the last day of school, Sam and Peter were way up top of the stadium announcing that day. They wanted some people to come up and join them and I went up there to meet them. They wanted me to do my rap for everybody from Center School. Everyone liked my rap and thought I was very cool for doing it. They wanted me to do some more rap and they enjoyed it a lot. I practiced memorizing my rap lyrics that I wrote; so I could get good at it. My stage name was D.T. Cartell, that name didn't help me at all. So, I changed

Alexander is bowling at Roxbury Lanes in West Seattle on December 2011.

it to Fantasy A; which was the name that sounded better. Hip Hop Club was my favorite program that I went to.

I'm always into going bowling; my sister is into bowling too. We joined the bowling league at Skyway Park Bowl on May 2010; it was so fun. I go to all the bowling alleys around everywhere to go bowling. I asked my friends, Sam, Peter, and Tuuli if they wanted to go bowling with me; they said they would. I remember how good I was at bowling; it was a great experience. Sometimes I was good at bowling; but I was bad at bowling and I was getting used to it. I got a few strikes when I was good at bowling. My friends, Sam, Peter, Tuuli, and Maya just showed up for bowling; I was really glad that they made it there. They saw me bowl and thought I did well. They always like to go bowling too. On December 2011, I had a friend named Andrea; she's really nice, beautiful and cool. I asked her if she wanted to go bowling with me, she said she would like to come. I brought LG with me to meet Andrea at Roxbury Lanes in West Seattle. Andrea came to bowl with me and we had a great time. Andrea and I are best friends and we like to talk all the time. Bowling is my favorite thing to do for fun.

When I was young, I liked to run a lot. But the problem was, I ran down the steps and fell on them. I was crying when I felt the pain. I have to be careful where I run, if I trip on something or a rock. I had a lot of accidents when I was a child; I don't like it when that happens. At age 12, I was outside in the rain playing around, I was running also. When I did that, I slipped and fell down a little hard; I got a bump in my leg. I went inside of my house and my mom put something on my leg, so it wouldn't get infected and put a Band-Aid on it. I always like to run faster, people see me doing that. They think I can run faster; it makes me lose my energy when I don't pace myself. Before I turned 17, I was at my house taking a shower and I checked the time; I didn't know it was getting late for me to catch the 106 that morning to go to the church. I ran as fast as I could so I wouldn't miss the bus. At the bad moment, I slipped and fell on the ground; it was raining. I started to cry very hard when I felt a terrible pain. My knee was bleeding a bit, so was my elbow, my hand, and my forehead had a tiny bump. My dad drove me to the store to get some bandages before he took me to church. During that night, I accidentally stepped on the toothpick; it was really unexpected when that came. I took it out and it hurts really badly. I had too many accidents that happened to me before; it was really hard for me to deal with. I still run fast though, but I always have to be careful of where I go and watch out for things. I really love running fast.

I go to the library all the time when I can't think of anything else. The libraries I go to are Skyway Library, Rainier Beach Library, Columbia Library, Central Library, Kent Library, Douglas-Truth Library, Renton Library, Bellevue Library, and all other libraries around. Sometimes I like to read books, but not often. I usually like to spend time on the computer and research on news, history, Wikipedia, and many more. I go to the library every single day to go on the computer and check out a laptop. I really like to use computers and I already know everything about using them. I type stories, poems, and everything when I print them out. I also like to contact people and my friends on Facebook, Twitter, Gmail, and Skype. I used to contact people on MySpace, but not anymore, I stopped going on there. My friend LG likes to go to the library too; he goes there all the time like me. People always go to the library to read books and use the computers. I check out books, read them, and send them back on the due date. It's really important for me to read my books all the time before I start doing something. I like go to the library to sit and relax.

Whenever I think of something, I always like to call up my old best friends and neighbors, John and Gary. I first met them when I was at Dimmitt Middle School. They're really cool buddies and they become so happy when I come to visit them. I also met their sister, Dalina; she's very nice and beautiful. Every time they are busy with stuff and work; I don't call or text them too much. My friend John helps me with filling out an application for getting a job at Family Fun Center. I usually visit their sister Dalina, which is my other friend; I really like their sister a lot. I got Malina gifts and she likes them a lot. I really enjoyed visiting John, Gary, and Dalina at their house. I was walking around the whole neighborhood, I went to my other friend's house, and her name is Monica. She's really nice, awesome, and great; I met her when we were little. I met her parents and brothers; they are so cool and great. I went to Lakeridge Elementary with

There is Alex, wearing his Santa hat on Christmas Day.

Monica and her brother; they also went to Dimmitt Middle School with me. I like spending time with my friend Monica, I think about her when I do things. We like to take pictures of ourselves and things.

My favorite holidays are Thanksgiving and Christmas. I love to spend the holidays with my family every year. I wasn't naughty when I was a little kid, not all the time but sometimes. I like opening presents during Christmas Day. On December 2009 during Christmas Eve, LG and I went to hang out at Downtown Seattle. I wear my Santa hat every Christmas; people say I'm Santa's helper. I love to celebrate holidays like this. During one Thanksgiving, I went to my aunt's house every year; also during Christmas. I ate lots of food on Thanksgiving Day, so did my family. I noticed that Santa is St. Nick; I've always wanted to be like St. Nick. On December 2011, LG and I made a Christmas episode of "The Alex & the Star Show. I used to play in the snow when I was a young child; snow was fun for me. My sister and I had a snowball fight together, it was really fun. Something I know about the holidays is I'll be enjoying them in my dreams.

I'm into taking pictures; I really like doing that. I look at the pictures that my family took way back in the old days. I remember those times, when I see it on my mind. Good pictures bring me great memories. I first started taking pictures when I was 11; I was interested in this hobby. I like to take pictures of myself, my family, my friends, the city, the lakes, and everything else. All of my friends like to take pictures as well. My teacher, Mr. Massie gave me a digital camera as a graduation gift; it was very nice of him. I uploaded the pictures on the computer and put them on CD, if people wanted a copy. Some of my friends liked the pictures I took; they thought they were very inspirational and interesting. I really love taking pictures of things I like; those things will give me the best memories of all.

Photography of Alexander L. Hubbard from Childhood to Young Adulthood

That's me wearing a brave crusader costume on Halloween 2011.

That's me and my Andrea at Roxbury Lanes in West Seattle; we have a great time bowling together.

This is my first book and play I wrote since February 2011.

That's me starting to bowl at Skyway Park Bowl on September 2011.

I'm always into Sparklers on the 4th of July in 2012; I really love fireworks!

That's me wearing my wizard hat at The Center School.

I got myself some packs of chocolates from my neighbor on Valentine's Day 2012.

I was very surprised; I didn't know that I got a Student Excellence Award. It really made my day look fabulous.

I was looking at the view of Downtown Seattle from Alki Beach.

I was also looking at the view of Downtown Seattle from Gasworks Park.

I won these tickets when I was playing games for my 18th Birthday Party at Family Fun Center.

I made those wonderful Oreo cupcakes for everybody I know at The Center School, I love making them.

This is me when I was a senior at The Center School September 2010.

This is me when I was a freshman at Cleveland High School; I received an Honor Roll Award on June 2008.

That's me when I was a king with my swords, but they're fake.

That's me wearing my graduation gown for The Center
School graduation.
That was me during the 8th grade last day of school at
Eckstein Middle School.

I was three years old when I pretend that I was driving my dad's truck.

Sorry about this, I picked this picture that was messed up and weird, that was me when I was nine years old at Seward Park.

That's my old substitute teacher and me with the students of Cleveland High School.

That's my old friend Kaila and me at Cleveland High School gym in June 2008.

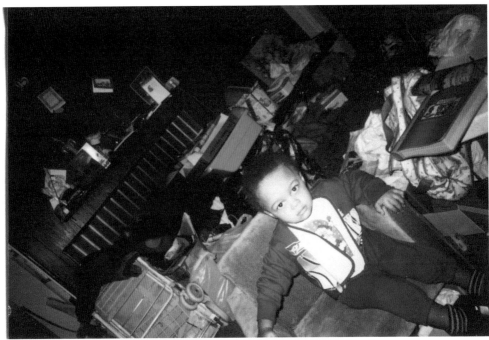

At age two, I was sitting on the chair relaxing.

I got all dressed up for my grandpa's funeral.

That's my 6th grade school picture when I was at Dimmitt Middle School.

That was me when I was wearing a crown I made for being king.

That's my old friends and me from Eckstein at Subway.

That's me and my old Center School friends

That's me and my best friend from Center School years ago,
Alex Diachuk.

That's my friend Gina and I at the Center House in 2010.

That's me dressed up as Michael Jackson on Halloween 2010.

That's my homie L.G. Shin and me at the gum wall.

I always love to go to Kerry Park on those nice days.

That's me with my camcorder by Lake Washington in 2011.

That's me at The Center School graduation ceremony on June 16th, 2011.

I was really excited that I graduated from Center School.

That's me and my friend Moses having our thumbs up!

That's me sitting outside reading the book I wrote.

22833267R00053

Made in the USA
Charleston, SC
02 October 2013